I0481629

Guide To Attracting The Best Tenants

Get Responsible, High Quality Tenants Who Will Pay On Time And Take Care Of Your Property

Thomas Cook

ABOUT THE AUTHOR

Let's start off by giving you a little background about where I'm coming from in terms of experience and knowledge. I've been in the real estate industry since 1980. While originally with Royal LePage, I switched to RE/MAX Hallmark in 1983, where I have been ever since.

Along with helping literally thousands of people to buy and sell their homes, over the years I've been involved in a number of other real estate related activities as well. For example, through the '80s I had a property management company and at times managed up to 350 single-family homes, duplexes, triplexes, condos, and small four- and eight-unit buildings, mainly for investors but often for people who were out of the city on a job transfer and wanted to maintain their existing residence.

That has provided some great insight into such things as tenant related issues, understanding of the Tenant Protection Act, and knowledge on how to design a really good rental application and a comprehensive lease. I find those things help today with clients who are interested in buying something that has a rental component to it — maybe the traditional basement rental apartment where the owner lives upstairs, or more likely today a downtown Toronto condominium suite.

I've renovated about twenty-five homes in Toronto, as well as building a triplex from the ground up in Riverdale. In 2008, I built a cottage in the Kawarthas that started with an uncleared lot. These experiences certainly provided some great insights into working with contractors, dealing with City Hall for building permits, and even on occasion going to the Committee of Adjustment or the OMB (Ontario Municipal Board) when obtaining a permit requires applying for a variance.

I find these experiences help with clients who might be interested in buying something that needs renovation or fix up work.

I can certainly offer advice and answer those kinds of questions for my clients — and many more.

For several years, I also had a mortgage company, which provided a lot of insight into mortgage financing and learning how to package the buyer's mortgage application to get clients the best possible rate and terms.

During my 37+ year career, my Team and I have helped over 2500 buyers and sellers reach their real estate goals. This achievement has earned me one of the highest RE/MAX sales production awards... the Circle Of Legends.

TORONTO'S REAL ESTATE TEAM
MISSION STATEMENT

Our goal is to give you such an exceptional home selling or buying experience that you will feel compelled to tell all your friends and family about us.

We use our time each and every day to its fullest potential, always remembering that our clients pay us to work diligently to get their home sold, or find their next home for purchase.

We strive to deliver more value to you than you expect to receive and to provide uncompromising service based on integrity, fairness, knowledge, professionalism and enthusiasm.

Once your real estate transaction has been completed, we'd be honoured if you were to refer our services to everyone you know so they could share the same excellent experience you enjoyed.

HERE'S HOW TO GET IN TOUCH...

Thomas Cook
Real Estate Sales Representative @ RE/MAX Hallmark Realty Ltd Brokerage

Mobile | 647-962-1650
Office | 416-465-7850

LivingInToronto.com
Direct | Thomas@LivingInToronto.com

Author | Ultimate Toronto Home Buyer's Guide
Author | Toronto Home Buyer's Financing Guide
Author | Free Government Money Report
Author | Insider Tips For Getting The Best Price
Author | Best Capital Gains Tax Advice
Author | Guide To Attracting The Best Tenants
Author | Guide To Downtown Toronto Condo Prices

Experience || Thousands of homes sold since 1980
Professional Designations || ABR, SRES
Awards || RE/MAX's 2ND highest award - Circle Of Legends
Charity Support || Over $115,000 contributed to the Toronto Sick Kids Hospital
Speaker & Agent Coach || Delivering seminars and presentations to the public and Realtors about buying and selling real estate since 1995.

CONTENTS

FOREWORD…

I'm excited about presenting this Guide to you. When I got my real estate license in Toronto back in 1980 my goal was not to sell homes but to invest in real estate. I loved the idea of 'bricks and mortar' and being able to gaze up at a three-storey home along that tall brick wall and knowing that I owned it.

By 1984 I had set up my own property management business and ultimately managed over 350 suites including single family homes, duplexes and triplexes, condo units and small 4- to 20-unit buildings.

It was interesting dealing with tenants over the years. Of course, the vast majority were great people… they paid the rent on time, they didn't cause noise problems for neighbours and no damage was done to the premises while they were residing there.

But to try and avoid the possibility of getting one of those select 'problem few' tenants, special care needed to be taken when checking them out and preparing their lease.

Taking a few hours up front to check out a tenant's credit, job history and references, or hiring someone to do it for you, is well worth the peace of mind you'll have once the tenant is in place in your rental unit. It's crucial to avoid any future misunderstandings by including all the right clauses in the lease to clarify the ongoing landlord-tenant relationship.

Over the years, as a tenant issue would arise, I'd create another clause to insert into every lease I did from then on to cover that particular issue. And now I've got a comprehensive 2-3 page 'Schedule A' that I attach to every lease I do for myself or for my clients.

In the last 30+ years, my focus has been on helping Toronto real estate buyers and sellers achieve their real estate goals on the sales side and of course, helping investors with getting their units rented to good tenants.

My hope is that this Guide will better help you navigate the investor-tenant experience.
Thomas Cook
Real Estate Sales Representative @ RE/MAX Hallmark Realty Ltd
Thomas@LivingInToronto.com
www.LivingInToronto.com

CHAPTER 1
GUIDE TO ATTRACTING THE BEST TENANTS

This Guide Will Help You To Know How To Fill Your Toronto Investment Condo Or Suite In A House With High Quality Tenants And Avoid Problems With Non-Payment Of Rent, Property Damage and Tenants Skipping Before The End Of Their Lease

Getting the right tenant for your rental property is the single difference between a profitable income property and an expensive headache of bounced cheques, illegal activities and property damage.

This doesn't mean that by choosing to become a landlord you are taking a huge risk. If you do your research into potential tenants properly, you'll find that renting out your property can be a very rewarding experience. As your property appreciates in value, someone else is paying your mortgage for you!

We've compiled a comprehensive how-to guide on finding that perfect tenant so your income property endeavors are as smooth and profitable as possible. If you are considering being a landlord, read on!

Why Do I Need To Find A "Good" Tenant? Can't I Just Evict The Bad Ones?

In Ontario, the Residential Tenancies Act offers little protection for landlords as it mostly exists to protect the tenant. This means that even if a tenant is not paying their rent on time (or at all), it will be time consuming and costly to have them evicted, all while they're living in your home or condo and potentially causing property damage.

Even the most obvious reasons that a tenant should be evicted (misrepresenting their income/work situation, conducting illegal activities in the unit and not paying rent) can result in an expensive legal situation that is time-consuming, all the while costing you several months in lost rent.

Even though you are renting out part of your own home, or an investment condo, you will have less say in what's going on than you may realize. For example, if you stipulate in your lease agreement that no pets are allowed, Ontario laws overrule this and you cannot evict someone for having a pet unless your condominium has specific restrictive pet rules.

This is why it is so important to find that perfect tenant – and they are the rule, not the exception – because solving any problems that come your way in a landlord/tenant relationship can be particularly difficult, expensive, and time-consuming for the landlord.

Put the effort in before you choose your tenant, and your time as a landlord will be smooth sailing.

Part 1: How to Advertise Your Rental Listing

Where to advertise

There are all kinds of places to list your rental for free, and you can also pay for listing space in rental magazines, put up flyers in your neighbourhood or tell your friends and co-workers to get the word out on Facebook.

Don't be skittish about using online classifieds like Craigslist or Kijiji, but remember that you are in charge of your rental listing and don't hesitate to delete any inquiries that feel sketchy or throw up red flags for you.

What to say

The process of weeding out bad tenants begins with how you word your listing in the first place. Be sure to mention in your listing that you will be running a credit check on any potential tenants. Anyone who has shaky credit or who has run into problems before will likely not bother to respond to your ad.

When describing your listing, be sure to answer any potential questions such as its location, the rental price and availability date, room sizes, what the view is, the amenities if it's in a condo building, estimated cost for any extra utilities and whether pets or smoking are allowed, etc. This will help you avoid an avalanche of phone calls or emails asking these same questions over and over.

Finally, be as descriptive as possible about your rental property! Discuss the condition of the property, the laundry and parking situations, which appliances are included in the rental, the parking and public transit situation, nearby neighbourhood features and anything else you can think of.

Don't hesitate to imply your rental might be snatched up quickly – that will get the response ball rolling!

Don't forget photos!

Photos will get your listing the kind of attention you want, but make sure the photos are good ones – ideally shot with a wide-angle lens from various positions inside and out! The rental space should be tidy, well-lit and clean.

When using your phone or a normal camera, take the pics horizontally (landscape) so the tenant can have a wide view of each scene.

A sunny day with all of the lights on will help achieve the right kind of photos - try to take pictures of as many areas of the space as you can: the kitchen, bathroom, living area, bedrooms, exterior and backyard, balcony or patio if there is one.

Part 2: The First Tenant Interview

First impressions

The first impression of any prospective tenant is vital. Does it seem that they've put in the effort to appear well-dressed and tidy? Or do they seem messy and unkempt? This can say a lot about what their apartment or living space looks like.

Questions to ask a potential tenant – what's okay, what's NOT okay

Landlords are bound by certain laws that dictate what you can ask to decide if you'll rent to someone, as well as what you cannot ask.

For example, you can ask if someone smokes, why they're moving, if they have pets, how long they intend to rent, their employment and income situation as well as who will be living in the apartment.

You cannot refuse to rent to someone based on race, disability, religion, marital status, sexual orientation, or the fact that they have children (including small, noisy children or teenagers).

When you choose to rent to someone (or choose not to) the information that leads to this decision needs to come from their income/employment information, credit information and background information (or information from previous landlords).

What to look out for

While your ability to ask all the questions you'd like is somewhat limited, you are free to observe the potential tenants for certain signs that can be major red flags.

These behaviours can indicate that the tenant may not be very respectful towards your property or may not be that perfect tenant:

• Tossing cigarette butts outside of the property
• Attempting to offer lots of cash upfront on the spot in exchange for skipping the credit check
• Not wiping their shoes (or taking them off) before entering the property
• Not having proof of their current address
• Being very eager to accept any rental property regardless of the size, price or availability

Part 3: Conducting A Credit And Background Check

After a successful tenant interview comes the most important step of choosing a tenant for your rental property: the credit and background check. This is a step that is vital to the success of your rental endeavors and should never, ever be skipped.

Obtain a complete rental application from the potential tenant, which should include their employment information as well as signed permission to run a credit check. If they aren't comfortable giving you their SIN number for the credit check, you can ask them to obtain a credit report for themselves and provide that to you.

Contact the applicant's employer and verify all of the information they've given you with regards to income and length of employment.

Ask for bank statements or paystubs for the last few months from the potential tenant to verify their paycheck, or tax returns to verify income if the applicant is self-employed.

Obtaining a credit check is simpler if you're a large property management company, but you can hire a company to run it for you for $30 or less. There are also companies that specialize in tenant checks, which will take much of the stress off of you.

You may not be able to ask the tenant to cover the credit bureau cost as a non-refundable fee on your rental application.

Part 4: Questions For The Tenant's Previous Landlord(s)

A tenant's previous landlord is one of the best sources of information applicable to your situation. This is a very important reference check and will let you know how you can expect the tenant to behave in the rental and whether they'll pay their rent on time. An even better one is the landlord BEFORE the current one... sometimes their current landlord is trying really hard to get them out !!

Questions to ask

You should be prepared to ask the landlord the following questions:

- Were there any problems with this tenant?
- Was the tenant unreasonable when it came to demanding repairs?
- Were you able to contact them easily when needed?
- Did they keep their living space clean and tidy?
- Was there any damage to their previous residence when they moved out?

Red flags

Unfortunately, you may not always be getting the most honest answer out of the tenant's current landlord – they might be happy to see the tenant go and will say positive things so you'll rent to them.

Sometimes tenants leave on bad terms due to a shady landlord or other things have gone wrong during the lease that weren't the tenant's fault. In other cases, the tenant may not have given you the contact information of a real landlord. Be wary of consistently negative responses or overly enthusiastic and positive ones.

When in doubt, Google the landlord or property management company. Try Googling the tenants themselves – you never know what might come up online.

Check to see if they're on Facebook – search by their name or their email address – and see what they're like.

Part 5: Don't Make These Mistakes!

The following are some of the most common mistakes made by first-time landlords when renting their home, condo or basement.

Being apologetic about strict policies

You're welcome to set your own policies like charging a fee for late rent. These policies must be mentioned to any tenant upfront and included in your lease agreement, but if a potential tenant appears to be worried about these policies or balks at them, this may be a red flag.

Accepting first- and last-month's rent in cash upfront

Some tenants may offer large amounts of cash upfront provided you skip a credit or a background check or give them the keys the 'day after tomorrow', but it's just not worth the risk. You can take the cash as their deposit (giving them a receipt) but make your approval pending upon a satisfactory review of their rental application.

Not doing proper checks

Yes, credit checks and background checks can take time and it may take a couple of tries to connect with the person you're looking for, but this is a vital step that cannot be skipped in the tenant screening process.

Collect your first and last month's rent in full before turning over the keys. And don't accept personal cheques! Get it in cash or certified cheque / bank draft form.

I've had tenants give the first month's rent, get their keys and not pay a penny afterwards !!

Remember, it takes several months to evict a tenant plus you've lost rent and spent money to hire a professional to represent you at the eviction hearing.

Not making 100% sure that a tenant is leaving when they say they are

I've had tenants give notice (sometimes just verbally and sometimes in writing) that they were vacating at the end of their lease. I've then gone to the time and expense of advertising the suite and showing it for rent.

Then, just a week before their stated move-out date, they contacted me to say they had decided to stay. Now I've got two sets of tenants for one property… NOT a good situation!

The solution… once a tenant has given their notice, have them sign the N11 – Agreement To Terminate Tenancy form whereby they irrevocable agree to vacate on the proper date.

They may still try to stay but the Rental Tribunal will very quickly give you approval for an eviction. Without that form being signed, you may be subjected to several months of hassle getting the tenant out.

Part 6: Creating A Rental Lease Agreement

Your rental lease agreement is the lifeblood of your rental income. It sets all of the terms for the lease with the tenant and will serve to protect you should the need arise.

What is allowed AND what is NOT allowed in the unit must be explicitly stated in the rental agreement, including:

Smoking. Is it allowed in the rental, outside on the patio, or not at all?
Pets. Do you allow cats and dogs? Just cats? What about hamsters or reptiles? Ontario laws will override this anyway if pets are not prohibited in certain condo buildings, but most pet-owning tenants will want a pet-friendly environment and don't want to cause problems with you.
Due dates. When is rent due each month? Include information about late rent fee policies if you have them.
Visitors. Is there a maximum number of visitors you'll allow, and what happens if a visitor decides to move in?
How much notice do you expect when your tenant decides to leave (the Ontario minimum is 60 days) and are there penalties for leaving early?
Do you want the tenant to be responsible for getting a replacement for themselves when they leave – with your approval of course?
What appliances are included in the lease, if any?
What utilities are the landlord responsible for, and what utilities are the tenant responsible for?

If the lease is not renewed, what happens? Most times in Ontario the tenant reverts to a month-to-month lease. Will there be a rental increase at that time?

How much notice will you have to give when entering the rental if you want to sell the property OR if you're getting a new tenant? Also mention that you are allowed to enter without notice in case of emergency.

If you are concerned about water damage, you can forbid items like large fish tanks and water beds in the lease agreement.

What alterations are allowed? Can the tenant change the locks, paint the unit or hang pictures?

It's a good idea to mandate that the tenant obtain property loss and liability insurance in order to rent from you... AND supply you with a copy of that tenant insurance policy.

A Final Thought – Outsourcing As A Landlord

Being a landlord and finding that perfect tenant is definitely a "hands-on" experience. It will require a little money, a lot of time and a significant amount of due diligence.

Landlords need to know everything there is to know about the Residential Tenancies Act and will save quite a bit of money if they're generally handy and can deal with problems as they arise without having to call a contractor, electrician or plumber.

In many cases, landlords find that hiring a property management company and outsourcing their responsibilities can be a huge weight off their shoulders, and it's something that you may want to consider if you're a first-time landlord or busy working in your own profession.

But did you know you could also outsource your search for the perfect tenant?

Toronto's Real Estate Team and our Find-A-Tenant Program can complete background, reference and credit checks, arrange for showings of your rental space and use their expertise (and experience with tenants good and bad) to bring the perfect tenant right to your (rental) door!

CHAPTER 2
AVOID TENANT PROBLEMS – FOLLOW THESE
12 TOP TIPS

12.) Avoid Asking For The Absolute Top Rent

I've found over the years that asking for top-of-the-market rent is asking for trouble. If you're desperate to get that extra few dollars, you'll often end up compromising about the quality of tenant you accept.

It's better to ask for slightly less than max rent and get more rental applicants who you can screen to get the most qualified tenant.

11.) Be Smart About Rent Collection

Are you trekking around the city collecting rents from your tenants yourself? Stop! Not only is showing up at your (potentially financially strapped and therefore stressed/angry) tenants' doors possibly dangerous, but it's incredibly tedious, time-consuming, and inefficient!

Instead, check out alternative options, from having your tenant INTERAC the funds to you every month by email to asking (not demanding) him or her to supply post-dated cheques for the term of their lease. If there's been a problem with a cheque bouncing, ask for bank drafts instead.

10.) Start Adding Systems NOW

You're just a "mom and pop" landlord looking to make a little side income, right? No need to hone your methods or organize paperwork?

WRONG. If your ultimate goal is to achieve more free time and not be tied to your day job (and yes, landlording can definitely be a demanding day job), you'll do yourself a HUGE favor to start building systems now.

That way, when you're the proud owner of 2, 3, or maybe even 5+ rentals down the road, you'll be able to step away seamlessly for that early retirement — and your business will still run like a well-oiled machine.

9.) Be Knowledgeable

To make landlording an easier task, you need to be well equipped to handle the problems that you will face. The best way to do this is through education.

There's lots of information online OR you could contact us... we've got years of expertise in dealing with all kinds of tenant situations.

Education doesn't end with high school or college — it simply becomes more important.

8.) Create a Policy & Stick to it

If you are running your rental business off the top of your head, making up the rules as you go, you are opening yourself up for a lot of hassle. Tenants will know if you are making rules up on the spot (no, you cannot pay rent in quarters) so having a written policy — that your tenant has a copy of— will make life much easier.

Rather than trying to explain why a certain action is not allowed, you simply can refer to the policy.

"I'm sorry Hans, our policy states that rent must be paid by a bank draft." People tend to not question "policy" even if you are the one who created that policy. Once that policy is created, don't deviate from it.

For all condo rentals, provide your tenant with a copy of the condominium Rules And Regulations from your Status Certificate package. The concierge and property manager will thank you for it.

7.) Quality Product = Quality Tenants

While this isn't a hard and fast perfect rule, in general the quality of your tenant will depend largely on the quality of the suite you are providing.

I'm not suggesting that you have to offer granite counters in your rental — but by providing a better-than-average suite you will set a standard for the kind of tenant you attract and keep.

As a landlord, your product is not only the rental itself. Your business is part of the product, and the way you run your business will affect how your tenant views your product.

Fix repairs promptly (hire it or not), maintain strict professionalism, and stay organized.

6.) Set Office Hours

Do you want to fix repairs at 10:00 at night? How about receiving phone calls at 6:00 a.m.?

As a landlord, you get to set your own hours. I publicly let all my tenants know that I am only available between 10:00 am and 6:00 pm on weekdays. Of course, I have a cell phone that will ring any time. Tenants don't need to know that, though.

When they do call outside of office hours, I will always let the call go to voicemail. If it's important, they'll leave a message. If not, it probably wasn't important.

The main exception to this policy is when you're trying to show a unit. I try to answer calls any time, but that's up to you.

5.) Know When to Outsource

Many repairs can be easily fixed. Many more cannot. If you are extremely handy with construction and tools you may be tempted to do all the repairs yourself. While this might be a good idea — it also may not.

Just because you can do something doesn't mean you should.

If your investment suite is a condo, there usually isn't much that can go wrong except for appliance repairs or maybe a clogged drain. Don't get trapped into replacing burnt out light bulbs.

In order to be a successful landlord, you need to balance cost savings with enjoyment. If you hate fixing things, don't fix things. Hire it out.

The condo concierge can often recommend tradesmen who often do business in the building who you can hire for those types of jobs.

There are too many ways to make money in this world than to be trapped doing something you hate.

4.) Be Organized

Have all the forms you need organized neatly in your file cabinet, have your procedure written down for all common problems (vacancies, repairs, etc.), and keep your maintenance contacts organized neatly for easy retrieval.

Keep current with your accounting. Have a clean office. These and many other organization tools may seem small and trivial, but they are one of the most important ways you can keep your business a business that succeeds.

Don't underestimate organization.

3.) Always Charge a Late Fee

It may seem cruel, but I **always** charge a late fee — and I make it known ahead of time about this policy. I don't know how many times I've had a tenant call with a claim of not being able to pay the rent on time but as soon as they discover I'm going to charge them a late fee — somehow they always seem to find the money.

Most tenants make a lot more money than just what rent is — but not enough money to live each month. As such, they must constantly prioritize what gets paid and what doesn't. By being strict with late payments, you place "rent" higher on the priority scale than other obligations.

The late fee that we can charge in Ontario is small but it makes the point.

2.) No Family / Friends

Sometimes I get a call from a friend asking if I have any place available for rent. My answer is always the same: no. Renting to family or friends is one of the most common but most disastrous mistakes many new landlords make.

I've rented to several close friends and even some family — each time I was faced with a choice: Get screwed over or lose the relationship. Every time I chose to get screwed over in order to preserve the relationship.

I finally had enough and "put it in the policy." No more stress from those relationships.

1.) Don't Be The Owner

Finally, my number one tip for being a successful landlord: **try not to be 'the owner'**. This is especially true for those of you who, like me, are peacemakers and non-confrontational.

As a landlord, you are going to face a lot of tough decisions and awkward conversations. When you are the owner, the blame is on you, and as a result, you will often make decisions based on convenience rather than common sense.

Instead, from this moment on, you are no longer the owner. You are simply the property manager.

"I can't move my 200 pound dog into this studio apartment!?"

"No, I'm sorry — the owner (or the condo building) doesn't allow dogs here."

Additionally, you can tell the tenant "I need to talk to the owner about this" to buy yourself time to think about odd requests. Instead of the tenant being upset with you, they are now upset with the mysterious "owner." Feel free to play this up all you want:

Me: "Sorry, I tried talking the owner into it, but he is a stickler for the rules."

Tenant: "Ugh, I hate that guy."

Me: "Yeah, me too…"

CHAPTER 3
SIX ASTOUNDING ADVERTISING & SHOWING MISTAKES BAD LANDLORDS MAKE

Now let's talk about how easy it is to screw up the process of taking applications and screening tenants. This is one of the most important parts of being a landlord — being able to properly select tenants will determine a huge amount of your success and happiness as a landlord.

So let's get onto the screw-ups!

1. Application Mistake: Not Asking ALL the Questions

It's easy to download a form from the Internet and print it out and give it to a prospect — but how many of those forms were put together by a lawyer (or worse yet, an editor) instead of by an experienced property manager or Realtor?

Naturally, you need all of those legal aspects taken care of, like proof of identification, permission to run a credit check, co-signer information (if relevant) and so on. But there's more.

You also need to obtain references that are not landlords or family members, a list of their previous (at least two!) landlords, including contact information (and previous addresses), verification of their income and permission to run a credit check.

Then — and this is just as important — you have to actually follow through and do the legwork that all of that information enables.

In particular, take care to actually call all of their previous landlords and ask them about the applicant's tenancy — including allowing them to fill in the dates of that tenancy.

Sometimes a clever applicant will put their friends' phone numbers as their previous landlords, but not many of those friends are prepared with details like the exact dates of their friend's move-in and move-out.

So we ask open-ended questions to try to expose these situations.

Needless to say, faking a landlord is an automatic "decline" from us.

2. Application Mistake: Trying to Profit From the Application Process

Don't charge an application fee… we're not allowed to do that in Ontario.

3. Screening Mistake: Not Looking in Depth at an Applicant's Credit Report

The credit companies do us this great service of condensing a person's entire credit history into a single number, and that number can tell you a lot — but it certainly can't tell you everything you need to know about a person.

This is especially true of tenants. A score can't tell you, for example, if their credit score is low because they regularly miss ordinary bill payments or if it's low because they have one huge debt that they ignore because they know they'll never be able to pay it off.

The people in that second category can make great tenants provided they have a solid record of paying their normal monthly bills.

In contrast, we've also seen applicants with acceptable credit scores who have nothing but collection accounts or consistent late payments on their credit report. Don't know about you, but that's not a tenant we want to manage.

If you're one of the above crowd who would go so far as to trust an applicant to bring in evidence of their own FICO credit score, allow me to introduce you to a cute little thing called Photoshop.

Yes, it's out there, and yes, people will and do use it to fake up all kinds of documents. Never trust a tenant's paperwork — it exists to be verified, not to be used as-is.

4. Screening Mistake: Not Understanding Income

The industry standard seems to be that an applicant must have monthly income equal to three times the rent.

But are they supporting other family members too (unemployed spouse, one or more children)? There's only one income number that matters: what the prospective tenant has available to make their rent payment.

This means looking at their take home income after payroll taxes and any other deductions, like child support or garnishments. Then subtract from that their car payments, student loans, credit card payments, etc.

Think you're done? What about utilities? You should be able to estimate those for your suite, but what about food, clothing, medical, etc.?

The point we're trying to make is that there is no perfect, guaranteed system, but you should put more thought into it than just the "3 x rent" rule.

By the way, don't forget to be on the lookout for fraud here, too. We once had a prospect who claimed to be an administrative assistant for a small 2-3 employee company give us pay stubs and a T-4 showing over $80K in income.

That might be possible at a big firm, but not the little mom & pop shop our research turned up!

5. Screening Mistake: Not Asking for a complete rental application from co-signers

The only reason you might be considering a co-signer is that the prime rental applicant doesn't qualify on their own for a variety of reasons.

Therefore you must do the same vetting for a possible co-signer that you are doing for the main applicant.

Often these are parents, sometimes retired, so you need to be diligent in asking the right questions and requesting the relevant documents to prove that they can indeed step in and help their family member if there's a problem in paying the rent.

After all, they are truly the back-up for the main tenant applicant.

6. Screening Mistake: Thinking That a Bullish Market Means Good Applicants

It's a common enough mistake — if the rental market is doing well, it means that more people are moving into rentals, which means that more good people are moving into markets.

When the market is on the uptick for as long as it has been lately, you start to get a little complacent because there are so many qualified candidates — but think about it from the shoes of a crappy tenant.

With so many good candidates squeezing them out of the market, renters with bad histories get desperate. If you think that someone using Photoshop to mock up a FICO score or using a friend as a landlord are unlikely, we've got some stories for you.

We've had applicants mock up entire employment histories, complete with excuses as to why each of a half-dozen businesses isn't available to be called for verification. The truth is that as the market gets better, the worst applicants get better, too — better at lying, deception and fraud.

CHAPTER 4
AVOID THESE SIX COMMON RENT COLLECTION & EVICTION MISTAKES

There's not a landlord who's been in business for long who hasn't had a tenant fail to pay on time — or at all. When it happens, the speed and consistency of the landlord's response will statistically dictate their success.

There are really only two types of actions a landlord can pursue: chasing the tenant for payment or eviction. Errors and mistakes abound, so let's talk about some of them.

1. Irregular Enforcement of Rules

One of the great powers that we have as landlords is deciding when to let something slide and when to really come down hard on a tenant. The response to a failure to pay, as well as the enforcement of late fees and such, should be consistently applied.

Letting things slide rarely turns out well and can be dangerous. Give a tenant an inch, and many will take a mile. It also creates a bad precedent that may be used as a successful defense in court, particularly if you do it more than once for the same tenant.

2. Waiting to Start Eviction

It's easy, especially if you like a particular tenant, to get strung along with a series of partial payments and/or excuses for no payments at all — and there are definitely (very rare) tenants who deserve that kind of treatment.

But what you don't want is to gamble with the odds or get strung along by a tenant you aren't fond of or don't think is being honest with you.

The easiest way to do that is to stick to your guns in all cases: deliver the 14-day N4 – Notice To End A Tenancy Early For Non-payment of Rent notice **the day immediately after** the rent is due, and proceed in all ways as though you're going to go through with the eviction.

You can always stop an eviction, but if you wait too long to start one, you'll end up in a less advantageous position for no real reason.

If, in reply to your eviction notice, the tenant agrees to leave at the end of that month so their last month's rent pays them up to date, **make sure** you get them to sign an **N11 – Agreement To Terminate Tenancy** form which commits them irrevocably to leaving on that date!

3. Accepting Partial Payments

You have to know the Province of Ontario laws very well when it comes to partial payments. Taking a partial rent payment may force a landlord to have to start the eviction process all over again!

Payment plans may cause the same issue. Check with a really experienced eviction attorney or paralegal, and know your options vis-à-vis the Landlord and Tenant Tribunal.

If you do, after advice, take a partial payment, definitely continue on with the Notice to Vacate process in case the tenant does not come up with the missing balance of their rent payment.

4. Performing "Constructive" Evictions

Some landlords attempt to force nonpaying tenants out by doing things like turning off the utilities (called a "constructive eviction"). This is straight up illegal in Ontario.

Even if your tenant doesn't pay, you are never allowed to make a home unlivable when there are people living in it. The penalties for doing this can be pretty steep, so plan on going to the Tribunal — that's what the eviction process exists for.

5. Trying to Shortcut the Law

To avoid any physical altercations with tenants, keep your distance and follow the proper eviction process using the Sherriff to deliver any and all notices to the tenant.

6. Not Maintaining the Upper Hand

When a tenant fails to pay on time they in effect gain the upper hand on the landlord. To restore balance in the relationship, the landlord must pursue eviction. The longer you wait to do so, the further behind the rent falls and the greater the upper hand the tenant achieves.

Eviction notices should be delivered immediately in the proper, proscribed manner – don't let any tenant excuses thwart this act!

Evictions have a timeline that must be followed, and the sooner a landlord starts that clock, the better their chance of regaining the upper hand in the relationship. This mindset should be carried forward through every step of the eviction process.

CHAPTER 5
TORONTO'S REAL ESTATE TEAM
FIND-A-TENANT PROGRAM

We have two **Find-A-Tenant** Rental Packages available.

Of course, there's never a guarantee... people lose their jobs, get separated or divorced or get transferred to other cities all the time during the term of their lease. However, checking out the tenant vigorously at the beginning will minimize the possibility of any future problems!

Package A

Some owners like to handle the rental showings themselves. In that case we supply you with rental application forms and instructions on what to say and ask the tenant when they're looking through your premises.

Once the tenant has filled out a rental application, and left a rental deposit, you forward the application on to us and we do our full tenant checking process.

We start off by calling their place of employment, talking to their supervisor and getting a bit of work history. We call their personal references and ask them a series of questions and we do a credit check on all tenant applicants.

Once we've got our facts, we'll call you back, give you a summary of our findings and get your approval to proceed with drawing up the lease.

Once the lease is prepared with our comprehensive Schedule, we'll forward it to you so you can meet with the tenants to get it signed.

The cost for this is $450 plus HST and is payable when submitting the tenant application to us.

Package B

If you're not available or don't want to do the showings, or you live outside of Toronto, we'll list your home on the MLS system to maximize its exposure. Showing access will be via a lockbox or key at the concierge if that's the way your condo works.

We upload as an attachment our extremely detailed **Schedule A** with all the clauses we've developed over the years plus our rental application and a list of the documents that we need to adequately check out the tenants.

Once a rental application comes back to us, we'll go through the same detailed checking process to ascertain whether they're a good tenant prospect for you.

The cost for Package B is one month's rent plus HST.

Contact me to learn more about the availability of our services to help you find the best tenant possible.

Thomas Cook – Thomas@LivingInToronto.com – 416-465-7850

CHAPTER 6
THE RENTAL FAIRNESS ACT - WHAT IT MEANS FOR LANDLORDS

As of the end of May 2017, The Rental Fairness Act (RFA) was passed into law as part of Ontario's Fair Housing Plan. The two main elements of that Act are to eliminate the exemption to rent increase rules and requiring landlords to compensate tenants if they want to terminate a tenancy for their own use.

Here are some of the details…

Rent Increases

Up until the enactment of this bill, any rental in a building that was constructed after 1991 was exempt from rent control and landlords could raise their rent by any amount the market would bear. Of course, some owners took advantage of this and were somewhat over the top in the rental increases they required.

Now any condo suite or portion of a house that has been converted to a rental are all subject to rent control.

A landlord may not increase the rent unless at least 12 months have elapsed from the date the tenancy began OR the rent was last increased.

Furthermore the rent increase cannot be more than the guideline amount prescribed annually by the Province Of Ontario which usually releases that number in the fall of each year for the upcoming 12 months.

That guideline amount for 2018 is 1.8%.

If you just purchased a condo suite, and it was not rented prior to your purchase, you CAN set the rent at whatever level the market will bear. From that point on however, the rental increases must follow the guidelines prescribed.

Terminating Tenancies When The Owners Wants The Suite For Personal Use

Over the years I've seen a progression where initially a new condo building will be up to 75% or more investor owned and, as time passes, and those suites are sold, the building slowly transitions to a 35-40% investor mix while the rest of the units are owner occupied.

In the past, when a buyer wanted a tenanted suite for their own use, or an owner's family member wants to move in, the tenant (who must be on a month-to-month basis by then) was given a 60-day notice from the first day of the next lease period. The tenant then departs at the end of the notice period and the owner moves in.

This 'forced move' creates a bit of chaos and inconvenience for the tenant of course and an added expense to pay for the move.

The Rental Fairness Act took all this into consideration and as of September 2017 now requires the following when the landlord wants to space for **THEIR OWN USE and an N-12 form is issued**…

- The departing tenant must be compensated for one month's rent OR be offered another unit that is acceptable to the tenant
- IF, within one year of the tenant being notified and actually departing the suite, the landlord advertises the rental unit for rent, enters into a separate tenancy agreement, demolishes the rental unit, or takes any steps to convert the rental unit, the RFA creates an inference of bad faith, and the tenant may apply to the Landlord and Tenant Board for one or more of the following remedies…
    - All or a portion of any increased rent incurred for a one-year period after vacating the rental unit
    - Reasonable out-of-pocket moving, storage or other expenses
    - Abatement of rent
    - An administrative fine for an amount up to $25,000
- This basically puts the burden of proof onto the Landlord to show that they are not acting in bad faith

This compensation **IS NOT REQUIRED** when the buyer of a tenanted house or condo wants to move into that space. The same N-12 form is issued by the existing owner to the tenant but NO compensation needs to be paid.

Above-Guideline Rent Increases

In the past, landlords were allowed to increase the rent over the guideline amount if there were extraordinary increases in municipal taxes, utilities, major repairs or renovations or any combination of those, although few one- or two-unit investors took advantage of this.

The new RFA, as of January 1, 2018, now prohibits above-guideline rent increases on account of the cost of utilities!

To protect yourself, a landlord should turn over the responsibility for utilities to the tenant in their lease. If the building has separate meters, this is easy... the tenant puts the utilities into their name. If the condo fees include utilities, then there's no need to bother with this.

CHAPTER 7
CHANGES TO THE PRESCRIBED LANDLORD-TENANT FORMS

In the Appendix of this Guide, I've included copies of several of the most common forms that landlords may use.

If you need to use any of these forms, I would suggest that you check online with the Landlord and Tenant Board for the most up-to-date forms.

http://www.sjto.gov.on.ca/ltb/forms/

If you do not use the most up-to-date version, and you have to appear before the Board, they may throw out your tenant application.

LANDLORD SELF-HELP CENTRE AS A GREAT RESOURCE

The Landlord Self-Help Centre is a great free resource for small landlords who have questions or need help with tenancy issues.

Their website is **LandlordSelfHelp.com** and they're located at **55 University Avenue, Suite 1500** with phone **416-504-5190**.

They'll answer questions over the phone or in person at their office. There are lots of resources on their website as well.

AMAZING FREE SERVICES AVAILABLE
TO TORONTO BUYERS & SELLERS

People always have questions when they're starting to search for real estate or when they want to sell what they have.

Toronto's Real Estate Team has designed many resources to help buyers and sellers through their real estate experience.

There are complementary books and reports to download and many free services available depending on where you are in the buying or selling process.

Take a look at which of our 'Free Stuff' opportunities is perfect for you right now...**FreeStuff.LivingInToronto.com**

HERE'S THE FREE STUFF YOU CAN GET FROM US

Exclusively For Toronto Condo Or House BUYERS...

Helping Toronto Home Buyers Achieve Their Goals Since 1980

Sometimes people start thinking about buying real estate years ahead and others jump right in and purchase a new condo or house in just a few months. Either way, it makes sense to spend some time learning the right way to buy and avoiding making costly mistakes on one of the biggest purchases of their life.

Our Home Buyer University has created several ways for you to improve your knowledge about the home buying process and how Toronto's real estate market works right now.

Enroll in as many of these options as you'd like and be all set to go when the time is right for you.

Perfect If You're 6-24 Months Away From Buying A Toronto Home

It always pays to get prepared. We've designed a Buyer University educational series with articles either bi-weekly or monthly designed to teach condo and house buyers about the home buying process in Toronto in a systematic way.

Go to **HomeBuyerUniversity.ca** and complete the Buyer University registration.

Timeline = 6-24 months before purchasing

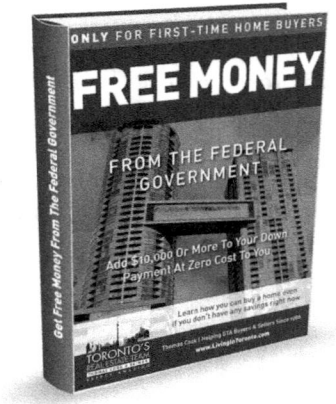

Create A Down Payment Even If You Have Nothing Saved Right Now

Would you like to buy your first Toronto

condo or house but don't have a large, or any, down payment saved right now?

Our Free Government Money Report will show you how to grow or add to your down payment if you're a first-time home buyer.

Download it for free at **FreeGovernmentMoneyReport.com**

Timeline = 6-24 months before purchasing

Home Buying Advice For 1st-Time Or Experienced Buyers

Do you like to understand how something works before committing to it?

The Ultimate Toronto Home Buyer's Guide will take you through the entire home buying process in a comprehensive way and help take away the stress of buying one of the most expensive purchases in your lifetime.

Download the Guide for free at **UltimateHomeBuyersGuide.com**

Timeline = 3-18 months before purchasing

Get MLS Listings Sent To You Daily Just Like Realtors See

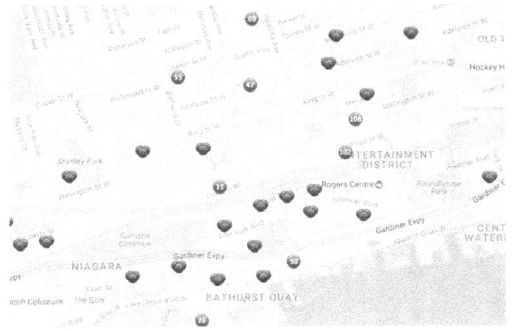

The customized HOMEWatch Program is perfect if you are several months away from seriously starting your home search.

Instead of randomly looking for homes on your own, you'll get information by email on all the new listings that come on the market in any price range and Toronto neighbourhood you choose.

29

Go to **CustomHomewatchSearch.com**

Timeline = 3-12 months before purchasing

Are You Wondering What You Should Do First?

Buying a home can be a confusing enterprise and many people don't know the best place to start. A Starbucks Strategy Session is a casual over-a-coffee conversation where you'll get your big and small questions answered to give you some terrific clarity about what to do next.

Remember, to achieve any goal you need a plan. The Starbucks Strategy Session is the best first step in setting up that plan.

Sign up at **StarbucksStrategySession.com**

Timeline = 4-16 months before purchasing

Look At Properties Without Needing Your Cheque Book

When most folks are just starting to think about buying a condo or house, they typically don't have an accurate idea of what they can get for the

money. They're often worried that they're too far away from the time they want to seriously start looking and don't want to bother an agent to see some homes just for the experience.

The Market Experience Tour is designed to help you get a feel for what's out there in the market in the neighbourhoods and price ranges that you feel comfortable with, without you having to worry about bringing your cheque book along.

This Tour is not designed to find your dream home... it provides an opportunity for you to get educated and find out what home styles, layouts and price ranges work best for you well before you're ready to seriously start your home search.

Market Experience Tours happen almost every day of the week... just pick the time, price range and neighbourhoods that suit your lifestyle.

Visit **MarketExperienceTour.com**

Timeline = 4-16 months before purchasing

How Large A Mortgage Do You Qualify For?

 Often people mistakenly think that going to an online site or having a quick, casual conversation with a bank rep to find out everything they need about getting a mortgage approval, but this is absolutely not the case.

The perfect solution to getting a full mortgage pre-approval is to have a private, in-depth conversation with a mortgage professional who will review your personal financial situation and offer options about the best way to move forward.

A typical Mortgage Consultation takes about 20-30 minutes and you'll walk away with a mortgage pre-approval that you can feel confident about. Sign up at **FullMortgagePreApproval.com**

Timeline = 3-9 months before purchasing

Here's A Simple Way To Save Time And Money When Starting Your Home Search

OK, so now you're ready to start seriously looking for your new home.

You've read up about how the home buying process works, you've been receiving some targeted listings from various Toronto neighbourhoods, you've been on a few (or several) Market Experience Tours to get a feel for the current market and your full mortgage pre-approval is in place.

The next big step is to meet up with your buyer agent for a comprehensive, in-office or online Buyer Consultation so you're fully prepared when you hit the bricks looking for that perfect condo or house.

A **Buyer Consultation** with an experienced, professional agent should take approximately 60 minutes... there's a lot to cover and understand and you don't want to make any mistakes or get stressed out in the process.

Go to **BuyerConsultation.com**

Timeline = 3-5 months before purchasing

Exclusively For Toronto Condo Or House SELLERS...

Sometimes people start thinking about selling their property years ahead of time and others jump right in and sell their condo or house within a few days or weeks.

Either way, it makes sense to spend some time learning the right way to sell and avoiding making costly mistakes on one of the biggest sales of their life.

Now that you've read this book, you certainly have a clearer idea of how the entire home selling process works but there are still a few important things you need to do. Our **Home Seller University** has designed some terrific ways for you to profitably proceed with the sales process.

If you are going to sell your home in the next 1 to 9 months, what you undertake right now can make a difference of thousands of dollars in your sale price, and there are some simple things you can do forthwith to make sure you get "Top-Dollar" when you do sell.

A Quick Way To Find Out What Your Condo or House Could Be Worth In Today's Market

Before you start making any plans to move up, move down or move out to a rental, you'll need to know a market value price for what your home is worth in today's market.

The best way to do this is to have us complete a FREE **Pin-Point Price Analysis**, where I can take a closer in-person look at your condo and prepare a very specific price for your suite.

This price will be more precise than the general range that you can get automatically from any website - and we guarantee in writing to sell your condo at the Pin-Point Price or higher in less than 32 days.

Go online to **PinPointPriceAnalysis.com** and fill in your property's specifics… it's that easy

Timeline = 1-12 months before selling

Increase Your Home's Value With Simple Cosmetic Fix-Ups

So, you're happy with the price you could get… what's next?

The absolute best next step is for us to do a FREE "Room-By-Room Review", where I take a 20-minute walk-thru of your condominium and make specific recommendations about which fix-ups or improvements you should (and should not) do to prepare your suite for sale.

I will point out the lowest cost, highest return improvements you can make to help sell your condo quickly and for more money.

Set up your Room-By-Room Review at **RoomByRoomReview.com**

Timeline = 1-4 months before selling

Sell Your Condo In As Little As 24 Hours - And Laugh To Yourself At How Easy It Was

Some home owners are sensitive to having a lot of people traipsing through their home or there's some limitation as to their putting the condo on the public MLS system.

If that's you, one solution is to include your condo in our "Silent Market" of condominiums that are not yet on the open market.

Because we generate so much buyer interest from our website, Facebook and Google advertising and other proactive marketing, we may be able to find a buyer for your condo without even putting it on the market… saving you both time and money.

Register your condo 'silently' for sale at **SilentMarketForCondos.com**.

Timeline = 1-3 months before deciding to put your condo on the MLS system

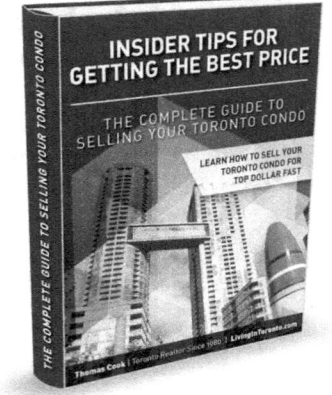

Insider Tips For Getting The Best Price - The Complete Guide To Selling Your Toronto Condo

By reading this book you're on your way to helping yourself have a successful sale and getting the highest price possible. As the saying goes 'Knowledge Is Power'. In this book, I will be telling you how my Team and I approach selling Toronto homes.

I've worked through three recessions since 1980 and now one of the longest stretches of market appreciation in Toronto's history.

So, I've seen it all... extreme buyer's markets and now extreme seller's markets... but in every instance, a competent, knowledgeable Realtor adds value to every seller when they're ready to enter the market.

Download the Book for free at **GettingTheBestPrice.ca**.

Timeline = 3-6 months before selling.

Get The Best Capital Gains Tax Advice For Smart Investors

Of course, no one loves paying capital gains tax when they sell their investment condo but it's necessary and you need to know how best to avoid over paying when it comes time to report your sale.

To create this Best Capital Gains Tax Advice report, I interviewed a tax accountant from a prominent Toronto accounting firm. He outlined three major scenarios where capital gains tax would be applicable.

Download the Book for free at **BestCapitalGainsTaxAdvice.com**.

Timeline = Read just before selling your investment property

APPENDIX

Social Justice Tribunals Ontario
Providing fair and accessible dispute resolution
Landlord and Tenant Board

Form N4 - Checklist

Notice to End a Tenancy Early for Non-payment of Rent

Before you serve the attached notice to your tenant(s), make sure you can answer **YES** to each of the following questions. If not, your notice may be invalid. If you file an application to the Landlord and Tenant Board based on an invalid notice, your application may be dismissed and you will have to start over.

☐ **Have you waited until the day after the rent was due to give this notice to the tenant?**

Your tenant has until midnight on the day that rent is due to pay you the rent. Make sure you wait until the day after the rent was due before you give the tenant this notice.

☐ **Did you fill in the correct termination date?**

If your tenant pays rent by the month or year, you must give **at least 14 days** notice. If your tenant pays rent by the **day** or **week**, you must give **at least 7 days** notice.

When counting the days, do not include the date you are giving the notice to the tenant. For example, if you give the notice to the tenant by hand on March 3rd, the first day of the 14-day notice period is March 4th; in this example, the earliest termination date would be March 17th. **If you are giving the notice to the tenant by mail or courier, you have to add extra days in calculating the termination date.** Read the Instructions to this form to see how many days you have to add.

☐ **Did you name each tenant who is in possession of the rental unit?**

If there is more than one tenant in possession of the rental unit, fill in the names of all the tenants on the notice. Make sure you spell each tenant's name correctly. You must give **each tenant** a copy of this notice.

☐ **Did you fill in the complete address of the rental unit?**

Be sure that you have provided the full address - be sure to also identify the correct rental unit and provide the postal code.

☐ **Did you check your math?**

Make sure you have correctly calculated the amount you believe the tenant owes. Check the calculations in the table on page 2 to be sure the Total Rent Owing is correct. Then check that this amount matches the amount you put in the box on page 1.

☐ **Did you include only rent amounts?**

This form is only for non-payment of **rent**. Rent includes the basic rent for the rental unit, plus any amount the tenant pays you separately for services (such as parking). If the tenant is paying all or a portion of a utility bill directly to the utility company or indirectly through the landlord, this is not considered rent. See the Instructions for more information.

You should **not** use this form to ask the tenant to pay amounts other than rent (such as the last month's rent deposit or an NSF cheque charge).

☐ **Did you sign and date the notice?**

If you don't, the notice may be invalid.

You should remove this checklist before you give the tenant the notice.

Notice to End your Tenancy
For Non-payment of Rent
N4

To: (Tenant's name) include all tenant names	From: (Landlord's name)

Address of the Rental Unit:

This is a legal notice that could lead to you being evicted from your home.

The following information is from your landlord

I am giving you this notice because I believe you owe me $ [   ] . [   ]   **in rent.**

See the table on the next page for an explanation of how I calculated this amount.

I can apply to the Board to have you evicted if you do not:

- **pay this amount by** [/   /   ] . This is called the termination date.
  dd/mm/yyyy

Or

- **move out by the termination date.**

If another rent payment becomes due on or before the date you make the above payment to your landlord, you must also pay this extra amount.

WHAT YOU NEED TO KNOW

The following information is provided by the Landlord and Tenant Board

The termination date
The date that the landlord gives you in this notice to pay or move out must be at least:
- 14 days after the landlord gives you the notice, if you rent by the month or year, or
- 7 days after the landlord gives you the notice, if you rent by the day or week.

What if you agree with the notice?
If you agree that you owe the amount that the landlord is claiming, you should pay this amount by the termination date in this notice. If you do so, the landlord cannot apply to the Board to evict you based on this notice.

If you do not pay the amount owing, you do not have to move out. However, the landlord can apply to the Board to evict you. If the landlord applies to the Board to evict you and the Board orders the eviction, you will likely have to pay the landlord's filing fee, in addition to what you owe.

What if you disagree with the notice?
You do not have to move out if you disagree with this notice. You could talk to your landlord. You may also want to get legal advice. If you cannot work things out, the landlord may apply to the Board for an order to evict you. The Board will schedule a hearing where you can explain why you disagree.

What if you move out?
If you move out by the termination date in this notice, your tenancy will end on the termination date. However, you may still owe money to your landlord. Your landlord will not be able to apply to the Board but they may still take you to Court for this money.

Page 1 of 2

How will you know if the landlord applies to the Board? The earliest date that the landlord can apply to the Board is the day after the termination date in this notice. If the landlord does apply, the Board will schedule a hearing and send you a copy of the application and the *Notice of Hearing*.

What you can do if the landlord applies to the Board
- Talk to your landlord about working out a payment plan.
- Go to the hearing where you can respond to the claims your landlord makes in the application; in most cases, before the hearing starts you can also talk to a Board mediator about mediating a payment plan.
- Get legal advice immediately; you may be eligible for legal aid services.

How to get more information For more information about this notice or about your rights, you can contact the Landlord and Tenant Board. You can reach the Board by phone at **416-645-8080** or **1-888-332-3234**. You can also visit the Board's website at www.LTB.gov.on.ca.

The following information is from your landlord

This table is completed by the landlord to show how they calculated the total amount of rent claimed on page 1:

Rent Period From: (dd/mm/yyyy)	To: (dd/mm/yyyy)	Rent Charged $	Rent Paid $	Rent Owing $
/ /	/ /	.	.	.
/ /	/ /	.	.	.
/ /	/ /	.	.	.
			Total Rent Owing $	.

Signature ○ Landlord ○ Representative

First Name

Last Name

Phone Number
(   )   -

Signature

Date (dd/mm/yyyy)

Representative Information (if applicable)

Name	LSUC #	Company Name (if applicable)
Mailing Address		Phone Number
Municipality (City, Town, etc.)	Province	Postal Code	Fax Number

Page 2 of 2

Social Justice Tribunals Ontario

Providing fair and accessible dispute resolution

Landlord and Tenant Board

Form N12

Notice to End your Tenancy Because the Landlord, a Purchaser or a Family Member Requires the Rental Unit

Instructions

April 1, 2015

SECTION A When to use this notice

You can give this notice to the tenant for either of the following reasons:

- **Reason 1:** You, a member of your immediate family or a person who provides or will provide care services to you or a member of your immediate family wants to move into the rental unit.

- **Reason 2:** The purchaser, a member of the purchaser's immediate family or a person who provides or will provide care services to the purchaser or a member of the purchaser's immediate family wants to move into the rental unit.

Giving this notice is the first step in evicting a tenant for the above reasons. See Section D below for information about what happens after you give this notice to your tenant.

You cannot give this notice for any of the above reasons if:

- the complex has been converted to a condominium and the tenant lived in the rental unit on the date the complex was registered as a condominium, the complex is proposed to be converted to a condominium and the tenant lived in the rental unit on the day the agreement of purchase and sale was entered into.

- the complex was severed and the tenant lived in the rental unit at the time consent to the severance was given under the *Planning Act.*

- the complex is an equity co-op (even if the landlord or the purchaser has a tenancy or occupancy agreement entitling them to occupy the rental unit), unless:

  - the building contains four or fewer residential units, or

  - the landlord or a member of their immediate family used to live on the premises.

SECTION B How to complete this notice

Read these instructions before completing the notice. You are responsible for ensuring that your notice is correct and complete. Follow the instructions carefully when you complete the notice. If you do not complete the form properly, your notice may not be valid and you may have to start over.

Under **To,** fill in the name of the tenant to whom you want to give the notice. If there is more than one tenant living in the rental unit, fill in the names of all of the tenants. Where there is a subtenant or assignee, you should name these people in the notice. However, you do not need to name other occupants, such as children or guests of the tenant.

Under **From,** fill in your name. If there is more than one landlord, fill in the names of all of the landlords.

Under **Address of the Rental Unit**, fill in the complete address of the rental unit, including the unit number (or apartment or suite number) and the postal code.

The Termination Date
Fill in the termination date. The termination date must be at least **60 days** after the date that you give the tenant this notice. Also, the date must be on the last day of the rental period or, if the tenancy is for a fixed term, the last day of the fixed term.

Once you have given this notice to the tenant, the tenant may end the tenancy on an earlier date by giving you at least 10 days written notice.

When you are counting the days, do not include the date you are giving the notice to the tenant. If you are **faxing** the notice, it is deemed to be given on the date imprinted on the fax. If you are sending the notice **by courier**, add one business day for delivery. If you are sending the notice **by mail**, add five days for delivery.

Example:
The tenancy is month-to-month and rent is paid on the first of each month. If the landlord decides to give this notice on August 1st, and the landlord is handing the notice to the tenant, the earliest date the landlord could fill in as the termination date is September 30th (60 days from August 1st and falling on the last day of a rental period). If the landlord is mailing the notice to the tenant on August 1st, the earliest date the landlord could fill in as the termination date is October 31st (60 days from August 1st + 5 days for mailing and falling on the last day of the rental period).

My Reason for Ending your Tenancy:
Shade the circle completely next to the reason for giving the tenant this notice. Then shade the box next to the person who intends to move into the rental unit.

Signature:
If you are the landlord, shade the circle marked "Landlord". If you are the landlord's representative, shade the circle marked "Representative". Fill in your name and phone number. Then, sign the notice and fill in the date you sign the notice.

Representative's Information (if applicable):
If you are the landlord's representative, fill in your name and phone number. Then, fill in your name, company name (if applicable), and mailing address. Include your phone number and fax number, if you have one.

SECTION C How to give this notice to your tenant

There are many ways that you can give this notice to your tenant. You can:
- hand it directly to the tenant or to an adult in the rental unit,
- leave it in the tenant's mailbox or where mail is ordinarily delivered,
- place it under the door of the rental unit or through a mail slot in the door,
- send it by fax to a fax machine where the tenant carries on business or to a fax machine in their home,
- send it by courier, or
- send it by mail.

You cannot give the tenant this notice by posting it on the door of the tenant's rental unit.

SECTION D What happens after you give this notice

It is important that you keep a copy of the notice you give your tenant.

You can apply to the Landlord Tenant Board (LTB) for an order to terminate the tenancy immediately after giving the notice to the tenant.

To make this application, you need an *Application to End a Tenancy and Evict a Tenant* (Form L2). You will also need to file a copy of the *Notice to End your Tenancy at the End of the Term* (Form N12) you gave the tenant, and a *Certificate of Service* to tell the LTB when and how you gave the notice to the tenant.

You must apply no later than 30 days after the termination date you put in this notice.

The L2 and the Certificate of Service forms are available at your local LTB office, or from the LTB website at www.LTB.gov.on.ca.

SECTION E What to do if you have any questions

You can visit the LTB website at: www.LTB.gov.on.ca

You can call the LTB at 416-645-8080 from within the Toronto calling area, or toll-free at 1-888-332-3234 from outside Toronto, and speak to one of our Customer Service Officers.

Customer Service Officers are available Monday to Friday, except holidays, from 8:30 a.m. to 5:00 p.m. They can provide you with **information** about the *Residential Tenancies Act* and the LTB's processes; they cannot provide you with legal advice. You can also access our automated information menu at the same numbers listed above 24 hours a day, 7 days a week.

Thomas Cook

To: (Landlord's name)	From: (Tenant's name) include all tenant names

Address of the Rental Unit:

I am giving this notice because I want to move out of the rental unit.

The last day of my tenancy will be [ ] [ ] / [ ] [ ] / [ ] [ ] [ ] [ ] **. This is the termination date.**

dd/mm/yyyy

I will move out of the rental unit on or before the termination date.

Important Information from the Landlord and Tenant Board

The termination date

For most types of tenancies (including monthly tenancies) the termination date must be at least **60 days** after the tenant gives the landlord this notice. Also, the termination date must be the last day of the rental period. For example, if the tenant pays on the first day of each month, the termination date must be the last day of the month. If the tenancy is for a fixed term (for example, a lease for one year), the termination date cannot be earlier than the last date of the fixed term.

Exceptions:
- The termination date must at least **28 days** after the tenant gives the landlord this notice if the tenancy is daily or weekly (the tenant pays rent daily or weekly). Also, the termination date must be the last day of the rental period. For example, if the tenant pays rent weekly each Monday, the termination date must be a Sunday. If the tenancy is for a fixed term, the termination date cannot be earlier than the last date of the fixed term.
- A special rule allows **less than 60 days' notice** in situations where the tenant would normally be required to give 60 days notice (for example, monthly tenancies). The tenant can give notice for the end of February no later than January 1st and can give notice for the end of March no later than February 1st.

The landlord can apply to end the tenancy

The landlord can apply to the Board for an order to end the tenancy and evict the tenant as soon as the tenant gives the landlord this notice. However, if the Board issues an order ending the tenancy, the order will not require the tenant to move out any earlier than the termination date the tenant included in this notice.

When a tenant can give 10 days' notice

The termination date set out in this notice can be **10 days** (or more) after the tenant gives this notice to the landlord if the landlord has given the tenant either an **N12 Notice to End your Tenancy** or an **N13 Notice to End your Tenancy**. The termination date does not have to be the last day of a rental period.

Ending the tenancy when the landlord refused to allow the tenant to assign the rental unit

The tenant can use this notice to end the tenancy if the tenant asked the landlord for permission to assign the rental unit to someone else, and the landlord refused. The termination date must be:
- at least **28 days** after the tenant gives the notice to the landlord if the tenancy is daily or weekly,
- at least **30 days** after the tenant gives the notice to landlord if the tenancy is anything other than daily or weekly.

The termination date does not have to be the last day of a rental period or the last day of a fixed term.

Ending the tenancy in a care home

If the tenant lives in a care home, the termination date in this notice can be **30 days** (or more) after the tenant gives the notice to the landlord. The termination date does not have to be the end of a rental period or the last day of a fixed term.

If a tenant who lives in a care home gives this notice to the landlord, they can also give the landlord a 10-day notice for the landlord to stop providing care services and meals. If the tenant gives the landlord the 10-day notice, the tenant is not required to pay for care services and meals after the end of the 10-day period.

Tenants can't be required to sign this notice

A landlord cannot require the tenant to sign an N9 *Tenant's Notice to End the Tenancy* as a condition of agreeing to rent a unit. A tenant does not have to move out based on this notice if the landlord required the tenant to sign it when the tenant agreed to rent the unit.

Exceptions: A landlord can require a tenant to sign an N9 *Tenant's Notice to End the Tenancy* as a condition of agreeing to rent a rental unit in the following two situations:

- The tenant is a student living in accommodation provided by a post-secondary institution or by a landlord who has an agreement with the post-secondary school to provide the accommodation.

- The tenant is occupying a rental unit in a care home for the purposes of receiving rehabilitative or therapeutic services, and
  - the tenant agreed to occupy the rental unit for not more than 4 years,
  - the tenancy agreement set out that the tenant can be evicted when the objectives of providing the care services have been met or will not be met, and
  - the rental unit is provided to the tenant under an agreement between the landlord and a service manager under the *Housing Services Act, 2011.*

The tenant must move out by the termination date

The tenant must move out and remove all their personal possessions from the rental unit by the termination date set out on page 1. If the tenant moves out by the termination date set out above, but leaves behind personal possessions, the tenant will no longer have any rights to those possessions and the landlord will be allowed to dispose of them.

How to get more information

For more information about this notice or your rights, you can contact the Landlord and Tenant Board. You can reach the Board by phone at **416-645-8080** or **1-888-332-3234**. You can visit the Board's website at www.LTB.gov.on.ca.

Signature   ○ Tenant   ○ Representative

First Name

Last Name

Phone Number
( ) -

| Signature | Date (dd/mm/yyyy) |

OFFICE USE ONLY: File Number

Delivery Method: ○ In Person ○ Mail ○ Courier ○ Email ○ Efile ○ Fax   FL

www.ingramcontent.com/pod-product-compliance
Lightning Source LLC
Chambersburg PA
CBHW071242220526
45468CB00002B/962